PINNING THE BIRD TO THE WALL

Pinning the Bird to the Wall

⫸❋⫷

Devon Miller-Duggan

For Pam
Sept. 2019

TRES CHICAS BOOKS

ACKNOWLEDGMENTS

"Finding Waters," *Pinchpenny* (1985); "First," *Calapooya Collage* (1989);
"Font," *The Indiana Review* (1990); "Awake," *Galley Sail Review* (1991);
"Fear," *Tight* (1993); "Proverbial," *Black River Review* (1994); "Vitae," *Hyphen*
(1996); "Quilt Square for R.H.," *Tucumcari Literary Review* (1998); "Visiting
the Old Ones" as "Farther North," *Hayden's Ferry Review* (1998-9); "Three
Paintings in the Rijksmuseum," *Confrontation* (1999); "The Woman
Who Was Afraid of the Dark," *Santa Fe Poetry Broadside* (2005);
"Giantess," *Santa Fe Poetry Broadside* (2005); "In the Morning," *Voicings
from the High Country,* (2006); "After 40 Years, Joy Trimming Co...,"
White Pelican (2006); "Caliban's Sister," *Whiskey Island* (2007); "Upside-Down
& Backwards," *Margie* (2007); "Skin," *Santa Fe Literary Review* (2008);
"Geneology," *Abbey* (2008); "Older," *Worcester Review*, forthcoming;
"The Unimaginable," *Hidden Oak*, forthcoming; "Painting the Beach at
the Edge of the World," *Miller's Pond*, forthcoming; "Brief Elegies for
a Mother-in-Law," *The Blue Mouse*, forthcoming; "After a Sermon on
the Road to Emmaus...," *A Time of Singing*, forthcoming;
"This is My Plan," *U.S.Catholic*, forthcoming.

Cover art :: "Three Moons" by Suzanne Sbarge
24 inches x 24 inches, mixed media

Book design :: JB Bryan

Set in Minion

ISBN :: 978-1-893003-12-5

Printed on 100% post-consumer waste recycled paper in accordance with
the Green Press Initiative. The mission of the Green Press Initiative is to work
with publishers, industry, and authors to create paper-use transformations
that will conserve natural resources and preserve endangered forests.

Tres Chicas Books
P.O. Box 417
El Rito, New Mexico 87530

CONTENTS

…For there is a boundary to looking.
And the world that is looked at so deeply
wants to flourish in love.

Work of the eyes is done, now
go and do the heart-work
on all the images imprisoned within you…

Rainer Maria Rilke
from TURNING POINT

FIRST

We learned everything on my brass bed.
Years after the Saturday nights
in the pink-ceilinged room
parts of me remember parts of you
distinctly as black hair falling naked
down the back of a white-skinned woman.
Dolls in fancy dresses watched
from the bow-front cabinet, calm
even when parts of me came loose.
Their arms and legs slipped from their bodies,
their heads rolled. They wouldn't go back.

SKIN POEM

The tender bits:
eyelids, lips, nipples, cheeks,
earlobes—places where the blood's
surprised burn escapes. The webby fold
between forefinger and thumb,
the rumpled knuckle-skin—loose, frail parts
we're born with that won't change in age.

The toughened bits:
heels, the pen bump on the thumb,
the tip of the nose
from poking itself
into others' secrets,
small scars from old cuts—
easy as geodes to crack open.

The misapprehensions:
By the skin of your teeth,
skin and bones,
foreskin, thin-skinned
getting the Skinny, skinflints,
under your skin,
just a flesh wound.

Busy old skin:
cracking with frost and browning with rays,
sweating in the summer blaze,
blistering where rubbed too much,
opening under knives and other blades,

black-and-bluing, flaking off, clumping up,
swelling and shivering,
and, always, the itch.

A Proposition Concerning the Flesh:
Shall one who lives in the mind
be called "brainy"
and one who lives lushly in the skin
not be called in like manner "skinny"?

Shall "skinny" not be praise
for those whose skins grow
like six-inch roses, redwoods,
prize cabbages, giant butterflies?

Skin vs. the Meat of the Matter:
The skin informs the brain
strictly on a need-to-know basis.
Consider for a moment that
the brain might die
and the skin still live,
but if the skin dies
the brain's good only
for the laboratory vat.

The Revision:
Angels are, in truth, without skin
and thereby unmarred by sin.
We shall seek the grace
of the Overskin, and the sky
will be her abode and her face.
The sacraments of the Great Flesh:

washing with water and salt,
pouring oil on troubling waters.
And after death
our loved ones will be given
our emptied skins, folded
in a delicate Fibonacci sequence
known only to the Skin Folders
whose hands will never be allowed
to touch the skins of the living,
lest they revolt against
the touch of the dead.
Their disciplines require them
never to touch themselves—
bathed by other hands,
sleeping with wrists and ankles bound,
and gloved except to flay and fold
what was used to hold,
and may contain again,
some flimsy and dispersive soul.

OLDER

And hungrier
when you undid my mouth
and took my tongue to swim with yours
in oceans full of fish like flowers,
my friend's brother, home
from eight years in the Navy,
picking kids up from school until
you decided what to do.

"Aren't you going to kiss me 'hello', too?"

And then down by the river in the dark,
your hands beneath my clothes,
like fish against a swimmer's legs, you pulled me
down against the seat, and taught my skin
to swell against your hands like gills.

"Tell me what you want. Tell me what you like."
Everything you did
when you undid my skin
and slid your hands inside,
took my tongue to sea and
left me dumb as beaches at low tide
without the surf to make the sand
pull water hissing in at every pore.
And everything you didn't do.
And more.

ELVIS IS AN ANGEL NOW

FOR FLEDA BROWN

With every step he takes, Astroturf appears beneath his feet.
When not in use, his wings fold in
upon themselves, like fans, sort of, but really just
exactly in the shape his capes fell into
when he leaned down to touch the desperate hand of one
who loved him so, who brought him flowers, her devotion,
all her prayers, who bears his name imbedded in her skin
and hears his voice and blessing every time the thunder
rolls across the velvet black of night. And now he has
no need of jewels, of studs, embroideries to pull the faithful eyes
across his manly shoulders, or on down toward his belt,
buckled rightly huge across the center of his hips, where his
procreation flared, or down to where bells swayed 'round his ankles—
no, now all his raiment glows in light and dark and heavens ring
and sigh along with every mystic note he sings, and every note
he sings is plump with grace, grace, grace, and
where he breathes, the faithful swear the air smells all of butter.

QUILT SQUARE FOR R. H.

I have not forgotten how to sew, or where to send to add you to
The Quilt. The velvet shirt I made you more than twenty years ago,
embroidered collar, ruffled cuffs—I could lay it flat, stitch it down.
I could draw, in threads, likenesses of your collected things: Ming
bowls, ladder-back chairs, Regency portrait, Federal highboy,
Empire table. Your body turned on you.
I could have sewn a void—a scalloped square the size of an antique
embroidered handkerchief you bought to be my "something old."
I'd have drawn my lapis earrings, the small black lacquer box,
a disc on which a man's voice sings heartbroken songs by Schubert.
I could sew enough of your particulars into a square to make
a picture someone else could see and think you'd not been lost entire,
that something of you remained as elaborated fabric, some trace
of how your hand felt laid in mine, so strangers seeing it could cry
specific tears for a specific man. Except, by doing so I'd make you be
among the public dead, your life sewn to a stranger's life. I will not
blur your name into another name, your loss to any other. And I will cut
no gift from you, for you into parts. I will not lay them down, your
name, your things, your death, among so many that I might lose you again.

FAVORITE PLACES

No matter which of them you visit,
the others come along—not for comparison, though—
just that love of place is a continuous geography.
So standing on a pier built randomly out
onto a clear, broad stretch toward the wide mouth of the Delaware,
nothing but the flat river, flat sky, flat garden state lying
in broad lines for four fifths of your view
and nothing but marsh and duck blinds visible in the rest of your circling
except for the aimless road you chanced on to come here, so that
while you're there, in that wind, you also stand on the Salisbury plain
with the whole gray sky massing on the northerly horizon
in a leaden boil underneath which the white-gold band of light
shines out exactly like shook foil and the standing stones
both darken and lighten at the same time, smaller than you had imagined
and heavier. And when you sit, your webbed chair plunked down
in the soft waves that flutter to shore at Mayflower Beach, waiting for sunset
and grateful for east coast places that allow the sky its huge breath,
you are also standing on the lookout at White Rock
in New Mexico, dry as the stones you stand on, while,
                                    several miles across the valley
another butte turns purple-red and darkens from the rain
as sunset rides along behind the thunderstorm and turns the lightning
the color of your palm when you hold it to a flashlight beam.
And at Chimayo, where the old priest feeds all those who
have the sense to kneel, and the stucco of the tumbling church
and the Virgin's healing dirt take both their shades of brown
                                    from the mountains
you have followed there, you also stand inside the diamond
                                    of St. Chappelle,
in the presence of absolute, incorporate *color*. See, they are here for you.

AMERICAN POETS

We're going to tell you, right up, the exact roads we've traveled on.
We're going to tell you what magazines we read, and where we read them.
We'll tell you which union our grandfathers belonged to,
the year our maternal grandparents married,
which countries in Europe we've visited and loved, what we drank there, but
the milk of our mother's breasts and our grandfather's cows never ran black.
Our cities are never histories. Our cities are usually detective novels.
We will never gather with ancient Chinese men
to paint our poems in water on city sidewalks
we're in love with angels and Elvis and not ashamed to admit it.
We write about our Jesuses, our Lua, and our Old Testament heroines, but
underneath it all, we're all Buddhists at heart, sitting around
waiting for the Universe to smack us on our heads.
Mostly we're all virgins. Mostly we're all floozies.
Mostly we have spent too long sitting at the crossroads
hoping the devil will make an offer we can not ignore.
We trail after English poets, but we pledge allegience
                         to One Nation Under Jazz.
History berates us; we know Hitler is our fault. The KKK is our fault.
Female circumcision is our fault. We remember
either too much or too little. We are either overtaken by music,
or we're deaf. We believe in magic,
or in fame. We are Puritans and outraged.
We all roll around in pleasure like puppies in the grass.
We sing seven kinds of hymns to seven kinds of listening
while blessing seven kinds of lightning in our several kinds of skies.
We love horses. We love summer when the air slides off
                         our skin in sodden sheets.
We love lessons we were taught, and the whips that made them sting.
We will empty out our psyches as if

poems are the landfills of our private neighborhoods,
then we'll bury you in everything we've ever read
and dare you to find a scrap of truth to nourish you.
You, you can't swing a dead cat anywhere in America without
one of us getting a mouthful of fur,
one of us praising the lovely arc of your swing,
one of us noticing how excited you've become,
one of us remembering when our younger brother
swung the live cat into the side of the barn,
one of us seeing the seedling sprouting from the dead cat's mouth,
one of us being knocked down by the cat's arc, then picking herself up again
and catching the next train that passes whistling by.
One of us is always in a kitchen somewhere
with a knife tamed for chores,
cooking one stew after another from whatever comes to hand.

THE FRONT DOOR,
or COLOR IN SUBURBAN CONTEXTS

Were it possible to ignore, for front door colors,
the metaphorical weight of each one, one could
then equate church-door-red with welcome and
traditions of the British Isles, but allegorical
equations factor in: let's say, sheep's blood on
Moses' friends' doors, or other, darker, breathing
sugary doors through which some children enter
again and again. Which *red* suffices? Which
color wards? *Door* itself is wood, head-high,
hip-wide, with holes for light and keys, with hinges,
meant to hang between one place and larger places.
Suppose a door—its knob and knocker, hinges,
weather-stripping, glass, and postal slot with creaky
flap—is not the only shield between you and all you
fear. Assume each holds back its portion of Outside,
and all the doors together keep it there, and all the
colors keep the doors in sync with one another
so that you can leave and then return, and I can
leave and then return and Outside stays outside.
Suppose, in metaphysics or in metaphors, all
the world's blue doors are careful intersections
keeping the blues of all skies and eyes, all reflecting
waters from spilling willy-nilly into each other.
Think: all green doors prevent the vegetative world
from vining through our thresholds, strangling us at
breakfast. Think of what black doors dam. Suppose
the door, your door, needs paint to keep the merely
variable air from warping it, and therefore you must
choose. And color, though itself impossible to slam,

to knock on, kick in, wrench open, or batter, still
has weight, animate and specific as a snowflake,
supposing it were possible to know precisely how to
find, much less to purchase, the white of snowflakes;
or, even to choose a single white, or know if every
color gathers there in perfect measure, if gathered,
whether each veils every other color equally,
or simply overwhelms the fuddled human eye
and leaves us searching for the door that lets us in.

AFTER THE SERMON ABOUT THE ROAD
TO EMMAUS IN A CHURCH DECORATED
WITH UNUSUAL SAINTS AND HEROES

Since there's no customary Lucy with her hands
all full of eyes, no arrow-stuck young man
in blooded ecstasy, no wheeled Catherine here
on any of these walls or windows, only saints and strivers
no one knows—children wrapped in kindling
or those few who speak when they should speak—
who knows who's who
unless you read the names
beneath Sojourner's feet, or Sayers' feet?
In glass at last, and lucified, they float on names,
so we can know who listens to us listening.

Today we hear of road—
I think of roads and sing inside my head
Frost's poem to a hymn tune that I've known
since I was small and knew
that daylight roads were safe
and all the roads I travel on at night
went where the forest witches hungry wait.
The preacher names the two who met someone impossible
along some road. I tell myself to listen
so I'll know the names.
It might be best to learn
to recognize who comes along the road.

It might be best to learn a name to call
my father should his ashes free themselves
and form in front of me on any road at night:

he'd beckon and I'd reach,
and we'd go on like that until I found
his name-in-death.
I know, I know, I know this place, these windows
and these saints' all-shining names.
I know, I know it's time to walk with them
and learn their lit-up, light-born, light-sung names,
but I know, too, I need to know that one dark name to speak at need.
You never know when you might need to know.

AFTER 40 YEARS OF BUSINESS, THE JOY TRIMMING CO. OF WILMINGTON, DELAWARE, HAS CLOSED ITS DOORS

O, walls of ribbons—
satin to bind the waists of brides, ankles of ballerinas,
picot for spring hats, velvet for winter hats,
tartans for the brims of bonnets, jacquard, grosgrain, holiday prints;
O, buttons big enough that Audrey Hepburn might have had
                              just one or two or four,
to clinch her coat by Givenchy, and mother-of-pearl buttons
small enough for christening gowns, Bakelite buttons for the fitted suits
of fast-lipped broads in Chandler novels, rhinestone buttons fit
                              for Liberace, abalone,
horn, brass, pewter, bamboo, glass, and children's' fancies—
checkered, duck-shaped, hand-shaped, flowered, star and
                              cloud-shaped buttons;
O, buckram, bodice boning, horsehair for flaring hems, and
                              china silk for linings;
O, threads in cotton, polyester, nylon, linen, rayon, silk;
O, needles for upholstery, shoes, doll-making, hats, or crewel;
O, folding scissors, pinking shears, tin snips, rolling cutters,
                              leather punches,
dressmaking shears as long as forearms and forged from sword-grade steel;
O, white lace meant for virgins, black for widows, rainbow lace
                              for clowns and girls;
O, sequins, rhinestones, crystals, pearls;
O, hooks-and-eyes in every size, grommets, snaps, and buckles;
O, measures, thimbles, threaders, rippers, pins;
Come to me, each and every, all and in one too-small, dusty,
                              treasure-hiding space.
The things I personally used: ivory lace around the linen collar—

                        like a cavalier's—
on a velvet dress in bottle green, spools of satin cording,
colored hemp, and leather I spun out and knotted into macramé,
the double-faced, white, four-inch satin ribbon on my wedding flowers.
O, solutions to a hundred minor puzzles, salvations
                              for a hundred minor gaffs.
Whenever I prick my fingers, I will smudge the drops on seams
                              and hidden stitches,
my fingers giving thanks in sting and gladness,
marking everything I sew in memory of amplitude.

THREE PAINTINGS IN THE RIJKSMUSEUM

I.

In one the slippery glimmer of a pewter jug—
I search for the verb; "sings" comes to mind.
I think that "sing" is much too loud a word
unless I mean the jug sings to itself.
What this jug has done three hundred years of,
sitting there, next to fruit that rots and flowers
passing their best bloom, is keep itself.

I find my verb: remember it, it's *husband,*
as in *husband your resources* (vegetables in the garden,
a hoard of coins, or just a shining spot that's mine).

II.

A *vanitas* in which a woman,
aged face pleated like her collar lace, cheeks
that Netherlandish pink, gives thanks to God
for yet another meal in yet another day, her face
all patience, gratitude, and hunger, while her cat
on my side of the table
climbs up the cloth to get her salmon steak.
I hope her prayers are brief,
recalling that my own are always brief,
and wondering if we'd pray at all
if we knew what we might lose
while we are praying.

III.

This couple sits together comfortably.
She spins, and holds her spindle up,
not so that we might see her threads,
but so she sees the smoothness of
the thread she's spun. And he behind her,
pleased that she is pleased,
rests one arm around her waist
and holds her, not for me to see his wife,
but so I see the comfort they have spun.

VITAE

Born between one moment and another of my mother's life,
doubtless an interruption in my father's—
in a Southern state I would not live in long—
but lived in long enough for heat rash,
never comfortable in skin from the beginning.
Educated more by what I looked at than by what I heard,
and more by what I heard than by what I read,
and have not read as much as you.
Honored by some who taught me and by few who touched me,
awarded once—no cash attached.
Published my distresses, severally: embroideries in black and white.
Previously employed in making wedding gowns, arranging
lush desserts and flowers—cutting things apart
and reassembling what I cut.
Seeking a position as the one who runs her thumb along the pink
sharp line of the morning's arrival,
the one recording the days when dawn comes on
pink as a breathing infant.
Seeking a position near a temperate coast
assembling the sounds inside some shells.
Seeking a position breaking someone else's
mis-matched, chip-rimmed dinner plates apart,
gluing shards on naked walls and hoping those who stop to gaze
see saints or shrines.

THIS IS MY PLAN

In the normal course of things, you'll die
before I die, older than I
and male, and therefore burning up your life
faster than my woman's body can
no matter how I'd wish
this body could vanish without you to hold it here.
Chances are we won't go down in flames
from skies between the place we live
and anywhere we go to look at paintings
showing other pairs—John and Salomé,
Danae and her lap of coins,
Apollo and Daphne, Adam and God, Adam and Eve,
Eve and the snake, old and affectionate Dutch couples.
And chances are we won't fall off some bridge
together, having done our falling years ago.

These are the things I'll never do again:
I won't eat lobster, sing the hymn called Hyferdol,
see the ballet company we saw on our first date,
ride a German train, choose a man's tie, drink English Breakfast tea.
I will not trim the beard and hair of any other man.
I'll burn the clothes of mine you liked, and
all the cards we played Gin Rummy with.
I swear, I will not harm myself, will not
fill my eyes with ashes, or steal dirt from your grave
to stop my ears, will not cut my skin
to let the howling out. I will not die.

What I will do, I think, is find someone to love
so all I learned of love with you
won't choke itself, or me.

LOVE POEM

Today, there is no person anywhere
I love enough to make a poem for, no one
anywhere I love enough to write into a poem.
Today, I'm thinking of the poems I could write
made up of lists of names of all those
I can't love enough for poetry:
both my daughters—the only two
acquaintances who've ever found the way
back out from underneath my skin
once they got in; some friends who've died—
I took them in and nothing came back out again
but tears; some friends alive and
full of words and world; some boys I
let inside who had no business
where I let them be; one man;
my ancestors, both good and bad;
the God I knew before I knew I knew.
Today, I love not one of them enough
to write their names, their breaths, their glances down.
today I only love the alphabet and all its clumps
like too-thick blood, that
shove their way into my heart and
out again to squeeze some air back
out toward my brain, which
will not love another thing, but will consent to ask:
If I cannot love enough, do I not love enough?
If I cannot love enough, is love itself enough?
If I cannot love enough, can poetry
be love enough?

LATE EPITHALAMION
FOR MIRIAM SAGAN AND ROBERT WINSON

I.

Since his death a tree in the yard
has been hung with fish, silver in the wind.
There is a Succoth canopy with fish,
ears of corn, small pumpkins, grape leaves,
bells and small drums the wind will play, gold threads.
Fish scales cover the altars all over town
glimmering behind the smoke, the blue door of the sky, fish drums.
Love like a fish hooked and thrown back scarred,
like a string of beads around separate wrists,
like a wound nothing can heal—nothing should heal—
love runs up and down the streets, searching for home,
running for the mountains.

Now, with the blood halted in its veins,
with ashes like the scales of infinitesimal fish waiting on an altar,
as if they were a million coins, love
remembers all its costs,
remembers all its homes,
remembers all its names.

II.

In the pages of the Widow's Book, these rites:
With a scallop shell found in an arroyo
cut the face of the dead

into your left palm at the end of the heart line.
Rake the ground where he walked of everything that lives,
burn it all. Wet the ashes down.
Paint your eyes dark at the rims as Ruth's, so that
when they open for your next lover,
he sees the black bearing down on your sight.
Bathe first in salt water, washing your eyes and your tongue.
Bathe second in vinegar; stay until your bones sting.
Bathe lastly in snow, shoving it under your fingernails;
stay until your heart freezes.
Using anything, cut your own name into your breasts.
Using rose thorns, peel back the skin of your face and write
his name on the underside of your forehead.
On the 49th day, sew closed the wounds in your feet,
take the thorns from beneath your eyelids and tongue.

III

Where the Sangre de Cristos rise from the earth
in walls as high as Buddha's breath,
The compass has six points:
one for each of the winds,
one pointing up as the land rises,
one down where the water dreams.

Where the sun is a four-armed cross
and the air pushes itself hard from the lungs,
some hand has cut the trees from the mountainside
leaving everything, everything fallen.
But Robert walked here,
and in the morning brightening

the air lived clear and he could hear the bells, and
the beat of your heart, and his own breath, and the fish swimming
oceans and deserts away, and time.
He could set his hand to anything
and make it grin, excepting this,
this dying as if he had fished himself out of water.

UPSIDE-DOWN & BACKWARDS

FOR MY HUSBAND'S STUDENT, RICHARD

Who found him?
> The linemen, on Monday. He spent Sunday there.

How did he do it?
> Without error or excuse. Thoroughly. With aspirin to thin his blood.
> Away from where a child might find him. With his feet tied in knots.

Why did it happen?
> The utility pole was numbered thirteen.

Could we have helped him?
> He hung upside down with a gun in his hand.

How could he do that?
> Upside down like the Hanged Man. Like Paul. Like a steer in an
> abattoir.

When did it happen?
> When he was finished. He wanted us to understand him.

Why did it happen?
> His mother wore scarlet after his death. There is an autistic woman
> who's made a machine that embraces her.

Did he have any friends?
> There is madness in the family. Not that he knew of.

How did he do it?
> Hundreds of people regretted his death. Something had to be killed.

Who found him?

No one he knew. He had written. Stripped his bed and folded his blankets. His dry cleaning fetched and paid for. All gifts returned to their givers. Strangers.

Why would someone like that do such a thing?

He cleaned up after himself.

IN THE MORNING

After the daily fuss of vitamins and tiny pills that
manage pain and slow the press of blood
against the walls of veins and channels of my heart,
carrying a second mug of tea, I settle at the desk,
sorting this day's list of yesterday's chores.

For the second time in recent weeks,
a lovely woman's long-loved husband died, abruptly,
hurt by a part that did its job one day but then refused.
He died, her message says, at peace, listening to a Mass he loved,
the Bach B minor. I heard, thirty years ago, that
Casals adored how headphones made the music
circulate like blood through his veins, and how
he wore them as he died, and so died already somewhere
other than his body.

Nothing, nothing I write could loosen
a single note from the silence she will push against
for months to come; nothing stays—
not husbands, wives, their musics.
I shy away from writing that, and say I'll pray,
and sign my name, and close my eyes.

TWELVE LINES FOR YOUR SHOULDERS

Here are your shoulders, which I love,
not so much for their breadth or strength to bear,
but for their perfect height for my arms' reach.

When I am at my tether's frazzled reach
and wailing, sure the world, which doesn't love
me near enough, is sinking in its teeth,

you reel me in and fold me in upon your chest
and let me taste your skin against my tongue,
your common brine, uncommon scents,

and all my thoughts come back
to you against my mouth,
my mouth against the pulses it can reach
and breach and thicken as they run,
which love I love. Your shoulders.

BRIEF ELEGIES FOR A MOTHER-IN-LAW

I.

The shovel in some stranger's hands
hacks open the frost-singed dirt.
This blasted March, the earth's cold as a saint's heart
and smells of pity.
The dirt they'll close this wound with
offers up more mercy than I could:
It gives back what it takes.

II.

We stand in rooms where the living wander
in to see the dead,
to see how she looks, being dead,
how we look now she's dead.

III.

Her hands lay quieted, polite among the ruffles—
a lavish corpse dressed in the only lavish dress she'd ever owned,
satin, and long enough to tuck around her feet.
Her face, arranged above the ruff,
is no more closed to us than when she lived.
Sisters, nuns, and nephews said I dressed her sweetly.

BERNINI'S LOVE

Bernini stands in the light and dust
carving his portrait of the flesh his love inhabits—
the face shimmering under his eyes,
the marble changing around his chisel.

A friend sprawls in a chair drinking the morning's wine.
Bernini, the friend, and Costanza will laugh
over the antics of a cardinal's secretary's lapdog
during that morning's mass.
The friend will finish telling the scandal
he interrupted for the Elevation:
He will tell Bernini stories about Michelangelo
in which a fussy Leonardo crosses the street
to avoid the stench and caking marble dust the Sculptor
wore even out into the world.

The friend will laugh into his wine.
Costanza will watch Bernini's face.
Bernini will laugh gently, wondering
Why anyone would wash away an angel's shedding,
his chisel opening up the stone
to pour into it everything
the flesh might ever learn of love.

AWAKE

Nothing in your mother's house liked us.
Then she died. Sometimes in our bed
you touch another woman.
I pull you back across the dark.

Three cats live with us in this house
and I'm the one with claws.
For I will consider my heart.
For I will turn and knead until I find comfort.

Your anger pulls the other woman back.
Lights spring off her body
where you touch me.

For I will tear down
a house where everything is toyed with
until it dies or gets away.

FEAR

The shark edge of a tin lid
slips under the tongues of children.
The dark edges in, all hands,
working under someone's skin,
lifting the skin of her belly away from her belly.
Severing the mask of face from face.
Soldiers foxhole between bone and bone.
Dogs and surgeons run in the streets.

Good mothers slit the eardrums of their children
before soldiers enter the house.
Good mothers hold their infants inside themselves
until they're re-absorbed.
Good mothers leave for new cities
and offer their breasts to living children.

THE GIANTESS

She's a wonderment for sure—

Hot-air balloons, in pairs,
give up their fabric for her camisoles.
Her skirts are rigged from circus tents.
She stole a dozen lives to line her palms.
Her pudding chins, from ear to ear,
choke off her breath.
Wheezing, she drags herself a yard a day,
no more, and eats a crop a day of sugar cane and beets.
Each breath sucks in twelve people's air,
and when her breath heaves forth, the scent of sweets
drops pretty women gasping in their tracks.

The problem is
she sweeps our children up and smothers them
between the folds of stomach, breast, and thigh.
The problem is our children run to her as soon as they can run
and ask to climb back in.

THE WOMAN WHO WAS AFRAID OF THE DARK

Some said it came over her in the womb
where the boom of her mother's heart
held her awake and flinching for nine months.
Some said that being born at midnight
from darkness and noise into darkness and voices
taught her. Some said that she believed she knew
the night is another tunnel into another womb.
And some said that she remembered her getting,
remembered the burrowing,
and the sharp invasion of the soft sac of her skin.

What we knew she knew was
that when the wind rustled the leaves in the forest
or the grasses along the road, she knew the sound,
knew that something waited,
waited to bite through the cord that held her to her breath,
waited to slice open her belly and crawl inside to warm itself,
waited to gnaw through her wrists and swallow her hands,
waited to sew her ear to its heavy heart
and refuse to let her die.
I say we should have never tied her hands.
I say we should have never bound her mouth.
I say we should have let her cut and eat the cord herself.

THE UNIMAGINABLE

One day, toward the end,
there will have been, in one chamber,
one mother who knew the end

before the doors closed, and found a corner
of the concrete room and held her naked infant
To her naked breast, nursing her

while they died, while others climbed toward the scant
clean air before the gas rose up. So they died,
one woman, one child, not meant

for human deaths. One ballerina tried
to make them kill her first and fast,
and killed a guard, and died

as uselessly as the first lame boy—the last
of his school to go, or any rabbi, butcher, nurse,
pianist, merchant, seamstress, just

man—last of the six. No death is worse for
passing unimagined. There will have been
children with eyes dyed blue, a son who watched his father burst

living into flames. There will have been
a woman who conceived, and bore,
and fed a child in secret. There are some

who will have survived. Imagine how

IN THOSE DAYS

. . . there were more colors than we have
and the flowers still spoke to us.
You could start again,
and in those days you could see
the ordering of things, the costs and reasons.
You could sit behind a boulder
and watch the witch call the wave back,
fling her net around it.
You could see the small moons
imprisoned behind each of her fingernails
glimmering as she pulled in the net.
You could see the children
wriggling like fish in the net,
their backs crusted with salt,
their eyes opening, the colors of abalone shells.
In those days you could shuck off your own skin
and everything it let you do,
offer it to the abalone-eyed child
who scented your blood.
You could offer your payment
and walk away from the shoreline
remembering nothing. In those days
no one had to remember her father.

PROVERBIAL

What doesn't happen is where to watch—
the mouse the red-tailed hawk misses by an inch,
the inept terrorist's bomb,
the absent third disaster.

The mouse won't wait until its heart
slows down again,
before it heads for shelter.
The bomb, behaving like a lover or a child,
won't do what it was meant to.
Quick! Look! Right over there!
You didn't see it miss you?
That's why you get to live.

CALIBAN'S SISTER

So ugly even
the beast-boy kept me hidden
then could not distinguish
me from stump.
He fed me on
what drifted close.
I came to look like what I ate—
blowfish, spiny urchin, crab.
If I bore a child,
I'd blind it
out of kindness.

While the pretty one and the old one
kept him fetching,
I dreamt much of the days
and all the nights,
always the same few dreams.
I dreamt I spoke
in poetry so green
trees grew
where the syllables
scattered from my tongue.
I dreamt my voice
made stars drop down to hear.
I dreamt my name
meant "mirror," "miracle,"
and "rarity."
I dreamt my breath sweet
enough to tempt waves
between my legs.

They've gone.
The beast-boy
searches under rocks
for something ear-ish
for his words to fill.
He'll turn me over
soon enough,
or dig me up from
where it is I hide
and all his fat, inedible,
unsheltering words,
he'll spit them out at me
all day, until he's empty, too.
And we'll go back to scratching
at each other's nicks and bites
to lure the crabs out of the waves.

RED NECKLACE

She remembered him by the scar—like a necklace—
ring of whitening skin around his throat.
>   *He never had a scar like that, but she is me and he is just as surely*
>   *Seamus, who I'm married to, and everything that happened just as*
>   *measurably happened once to us—*
She called him her night, and made him tell it over
and over, how the Coldnesses came from beneath his floors at night
and wound themselves around his neck to warm themselves,
how, in that winter we still speak of, the Coldnesses became so
>   inescapable,
they clutched too hard and burned themselves into his neck, and how he
kept them with him so that they would leave her be,
free of dreams she'd have to offer up, come morning.
>   *as when he married me and saved me from the lessons I'd been taught,*
She remembered dragging him back down to bed
between the nettle sheets she slept beneath and on
to keep her skin awake although she dreamt.
She cried, recalling how he cringed until his skin touched hers.
And, she remembered last of all, the waking up
among the small, white-petaled flowers everywhere,
covering especially the pillow where his head had lain.

He remembers how her whitish gown slid softly down
away from her pale shoulders, and the hem
pooling on the floor around her feet, the fabric whispering,
muffled by its own falling folds, whispering the song in which
red-headed children in gray robes carry fireflies between cupped hands,
and yellow-headed children in gray robes come bearing sweets,
>   *and later when he sickened and I sang and prayed and stayed with him*
>   *until infection left him free to learn to walk again and all the while he*

thought his breathing bed resided in a room that had appeared inside
  the parish walls of where we pray among believers
walking for hours among silent trees and the rustle of their parents' voices.

In another country altogether, all they had to hold on to was
  like ourselves, who prayed with us to call our story out of where infection
  wanted it to go. We're not these two. We are these two. I thought he would
  be eaten by the night and by the staphylococcal fury in his blood, his bones,
  his tissues, fibers, cells. I thought he would be eaten, and no one could
  tell me how or why.
how the swan-long necks of women crowned with clouds of wind-blown hair
seemed longer still, and sweeter underneath their perfect chins
when lengths of lace or ribbon circled around just where the dark
hands of the night had drawn away the blades.

ARIEL'S DAUGHTER

Man, woman, sprite,
flower, spume, or mist—
whatever got me in its
belly, bud, or tendrils—
it's gone, gone, let go from here
by the man/father/namer being
that walked upright and said such words
as held an Ariel-thing leashed upon this beach,
and I'm left here, a creature
egged or seeded in a tree
lullayed by bees,
suckled on the spit of hummingbirds,
delivered by dragonflies
already old, and dripping honey from my breasts,
wombless, willow-haired, six-fingered,
barren keeper of a fertile place.
The rocks here move on feet, the trees uproot
and root themselves on reefs around the isle
to keep the sight of ships
from us, the story-wrecked.
All alone with monsters,
flowery fish, fishy trees, wingy flowers,
I catch and eat still-beating hearts of birds.
And if I sleep, the dark draws in its fingers,
cutting off the color of my breath. I do not sleep.
I open oysters, slit their hinges,
lay them out beneath the moon,
watch them glisten at the stars,
then shrivel in the rising sun,

dead around their pearls.
I throw myself against the rocks
until I'm pierced
and beg the stones to let me
bring forth from underneath my skin
an egg, a sac, a pearl, some
thing with eyes to see me, some
thing I'll know I must not eat, some being
that, along with me, might make a population
for this place, that we together
might have names and histories.

MAYBE A GHOST STORY

After all the proper sights,
we went to see the dead at Pere Lachaise:
Abelard, Jim Morrison, La Bernhardt
and the myriad bourgeoisie of France,
among whose grand memorials the grandest
stands to all the fallen firemen Paris has had cause to thank.
But in the better neighborhoods
within this metropolis of dust,
the monuments stand wall-by-wall, and
roof-by-wing, and all, I note,
Have windows. Windows.
Windows so the dead
can see their neighbors come and go?
Windows so the toy-sized houses
seem normal enough
that Satan on the prowl
might think no one home to let him in?

On our bright lively day,
there with my two bright lively friends,
I thought that
were I much inclined
toward telling horror tales, I'd say
I knew why all the streets around the Pere Lachaise
had no cafés
and all the metro stops had extra stairs.

WHAT I HAVE TO REMEMBER

These parts of the story: There was a woman, and a poet, a bird, three seasons, a forest with black tree trunks and no undergrowth—only grass and light between the trees. The woman is white-skinned and naked. Her hip-length hair is, oddly, green. I remember that as a child I always wanted green hair. She walks naked through the forest even though it is autumn and the light is gray with the cold. She walks toward a cottage in the middle of the forest, roofed with black thatch, with black window-frames and a black door. She knows she can be warmed there. A poet lives in the cottage, which has a single room, wood floors, a wooden desk, a large stone fireplace. The poet's fingers are long—always curving as though to hold something. He (I have always told myself it is *he*) opens the door to the woman's knock, pulls her into the warm house, warms her, breathes into her hair, lifts it and lets it fall, curves the curved fingers around her shoulders, all over her white skin all through the winter. This is what the woman has come for. All winter, the poet holds the woman, warming her and then taking the warmth back from her, never lighting the fire in the fireplace. She is enough warmth for him, and he doesn't need to write while she is there.

Sharp wire bristles line the chimney to keep enemies and the light out. The bird—small, round, and black—ruffles itself in between the wires to reach the poet, who has been waiting with fingers curved to hold exactly that bird. Her wings beat like hearts in his hands. Her heart beats like wings in the hands, against the poet's face, against the poet's neck—all the breath in the forest breathed between them. The woman runs back into the forest, over the spring-bright grass, through the green-bright air. That kind of air has always made me sorry to be clothed.

In the fall, when she returns, walking slowly, still naked but warmed by her own blood falling down her back, the forest light crackled red through the leaves. I can see that clearly, and her neck, where her head had been, and the knife in her hand she had used, but I don't remember how it is that she still knows the way to the cottage, or how to walk or hold the knife. This time, when the poet opens the door, she throws the knife and pins the bird to the wall, through the heart, and then, taking the poet's hand by the wrist, drives it deep in the wound where her head had been and the blood boils the flesh from his bones. It was the hand he had been writing with. I don't remember whether she dies then, or what happened to the poet. The bird's wings continue to beat for a while, then it dies of starvation there on the wall, and the knife drops away and the bird flies off into the forest.

A STORM AT THE BEACH
AT THE EDGE OF THE WORLD

I.

Light blows in from every quarter,
soaking dune and grass together the way salt water furrows sand.

The tide slides off the edge,
giving up the boneless creatures to the gulls.

Way out, bruise-colored clouds line up along where
the sky begins to thud against the dark green water.

II.

Having hauled everything it knows across the water,
the weather rises up and shakes itself.

Gulls finish taking everything they can, cry off,
unfurl and slip the weather underneath their wings.

The horizon turns itself into a forest made of yellow trees.
only we are left to watch, and later swear

we saw the purpled sky spread out the line it meets the water on,
and go black, just there,

and blank out all the land peripheral to where we sat,
and boil out from somewhere

where there is no world but water, salt, lightning,
wind combing the beach grass flat.

Nothing taller than a huddled gull belongs here.
Rain in iron-hard drops slaps us as we run,

but we run laughing, stung first by wind-spewed sand
and then by stony rain—we can't dig in beneath the sand

or breathe beneath the water, but we stayed long enough—
reminding us our skins are still alive and welcome to contain us.

FAVORITE THINGS

I wish I knew what creature's shell it is
the sea wears down until what's washed up
is washed down to layers—so few that
you can count them all—
of nacreous shine no thicker than the toenail
flicking them over in the sand to
fluster and fuss with the sunlight.
I wish I knew what creature has been dead long enough
to turn slight and gorgeous as a jingle shell,
peachy, sunlight-colored, or, very rarely, seaweed green.

I've always wished for skin like that,
but soft, so I could shimmer and attract
and frighten whoever I wanted, including you,
and that the rustle of my skin against my skin
tasted to you like saltwater air.
But this evening I don't want you. I think
I want the broad, hard, flat,
simple plane of the beach when the tide's out and
the springs that send fresh water up
to mingle with the salt and draw whole
miniature landscapes of rivers and
canyons running into the waves, and
I want to walk where the beached rocks make
a Zen garden as barnacled, razor-sharp, serene
as a mermaid's hair. I can describe these things:
I am walking on a beach which is almost flat for miles.
The grains of sand settle tightly against one another
and even my wide, heavy feet leave only shallow prints,
even where clams and small crabs live.
Everything lives here, even the light.

WHAT TO SAY ·

They come scratching and tumbling up onto the sand,
a prehistoric horde of helmets, tails, fingery legs
accruing with the tide,
out from under the delicious dark weight of water,
washing up into gritty brilliance, the spring moon, Slaughter Beach,
Delaware, climbing onto each others' backs, spurting eggs.
They die, then, or understand enough to find the water.
The dead pile up, hills of rot and spent obedience to instinct.
Somewhere else, half a globe away, the same thing happens.
At both beaches, people arrive and carry horseshoe crabs back to water,
like farmers nudging stupid lambs toward the proper teats.
And I stay here, with no more idea what to do or say
about a million incidental, cyclic deaths,
or about a hundred million murders
or about my own grandmother, dead at 85, and
whose long dying stripped her down to bones and pain
and fragile courtesies, and stripped my father down
to someone who will die, and stripped me down
to someone who won't speak.

PAINTING THE BEACH
AT THE EDGE OF THE WORLD

I batten down a sheet
and sink my brushes into hauled-in water.
Then I wait.
The air's all full of salt and baking sand,
and full of all the scents of all the sex
the clams and crabs and sandworms have beneath the tide;
I breathe in and hold my breath.

The sun drops colors down.
The gulls pick up their prey.
The sun sloughs colors off.
Hermit crabs all over scrabble out of too-small houses,
gull-bait until they're safe inside their bigger shells.
It all goes on.

My brush grabs up the graded blues
and writes down what I see of sky.
A green gusts off, flaws out, I try to find its name before it goes,
to take it down in pigment.

Out there, somewhere I can't precisely name,
a storm achieves itself, sucking in the shades and shapes
it doesn't need to know it needs.
It's laying itself across the water
in all the shades of purpled greens and grays I've made
cleaning off my brushes in the jar.
Beyond this boiling horizon and these paints,
fish beget more fish and crabs more crabs and
plankton reproduce to feed the humpback whales and

other storms shoulder up to other shores, unwatched, or watched.
I know it's there, all there, and settle for some lines—
the horizontals of the water, sand, sky, clouds,
and hope to hold some light down on the too-small page.

GENEALOGY

If on the one side of your family
you have a grandfather you cannot recall
except to say that one prettily-lit morning
when you were too small to keep up
he took you fishing,
and the only thing you clearly recall
is the loveliness of the sun
fluttering over the galvanized surface of the minnow pail
and the tiny rainbow flickers of the minnows within,
that and his big hands closing the lid
on an old-fashioned red tartan round metal cooler
full of, most likely, sandwiches
packed by a grandmother you remember
a thousand things about,

if on the other side
you can recall one story after another,
about the grandfather who offered his cousin William Faulkner
a drink of milk from the dairy where Faulkner looked him up,
(you recall its name was Hollybrook Dairy,
the exact rich taste of the milk, the year your grandfather
lost the dairy in a fight with the IRS
and got Shingles from the stress,
and you remember you kept staring at his scalp
to see the tiny roofing scales),
and Faulkner asked instead for whiskey and accepted water,
if you know to say exactly how many years
that grandfather spent inventing invisible suspenders
at a Tinker's bench in his garage,

then will you fish, invent the invisible, or
pour whiskey, milk, and water around the roots of the family tree
and keep off any branch hanging over water?
And then how many names are yours?

A SMALL BEACH TOWN IN MAINE

Of course we swam in that *cold* water.
And no, I will not write the name of that small place.
Its hundred houses and two old-style hotels,
its fish market and produce stand,
its porches and six streets to which the same families come
year after year for decades, weeping every August when they leave,
these things all should be left alone.
For the water's sake, so cold that mothers zip their children into surfers' suits
every day at 4:00 when sun slants off and takes the warmth away.
For the light's sake, unfiltered by too many cars and
reflected off nothing but the water and the windows.
For the water's clarity. This year we swam with fish as long as arms
who stayed just far enough away that we could only say
they're speckled, brown and silver, dinner-big.
And yet we never mentioned them to any of the men
who came down every night, with waders or without
to stand and stand and stand and cast for fish
we never saw them catch.
Anyway, the water's crisp like apples, sharp like needles,
and it pulls your legs around as if an earthquake reached just for them.
You go in water there, in Maine, you know you've been to sea.
You know there's something always on the other side of summer—
When the landscape shuts back down and the puritan cold returns.
But now, in early August at the beach, you know your
nerves and skin cells are awake and fed by summer warmth, ready to go on.
And down here you know other things—the bayberry/blueberry/salt
sweetness of the air so scrubbed and seasoned you can sit
next to an open window breathing and content with nothing more than that,
or walk down to the shipwreck buried in the sand
where the creek slips through the marsh and channels out to sea,

the foundered schooner's ribs as clear and dark against the sand
as script across a page, and as mysterious.
Or just stand still and watch the rocks the waves uncover and
Re-cover twice a day and beat against sometimes.
Three boys, all teenagers whose names you never think to know,
spend all an afternoon at setting up the log that floated in,
upright it in a hole they dug and dug,
then take their turns ascending to the top and sitting there like hermits
until the sand gives way. Each morning the young father's out
and walking up and down, his bright-headed baby girl strapped to his chest
reading as he walks, just like my husband walked our baby girl at sunrise.
Twenty-four years apart, both baby girls are named, I swear it, *Hannah*.

It's not because you don't deserve some stretch of sand, some water,
or some air, some unbedazzled place like that small beach in Maine.
You do. *You* do. You do, too.
I've said it—what it is you'd need to want to find—that was my part.

WAITING FOR THE WATER TO RISE

What I wanted to be was Blodewedd, the Flower Woman,
capable of twisting men's hearts
until they told me
the long riddle of my death;
some enchantress, capable of taking
the hearts of Demon Lovers and
embroidering my biography in silk
on the left ventricle before they
thought to leave me. What I wanted to be was
Ophelia by Burne-Jones, wafting
languid and dead down any river that would have me,
hair and brocade skirts displayed to best advantage,
serene as a water plant,
and wet enough for any man.

GUERNICA

The *Britannica* lies open to Picasso's entry
where I've left it and gone on to other work.
My daughter, four or five or six, is stopped
and staring at the quarter-page reprint in grays
of Guernica. And while I think of how
to say what it's a picture of, she points and says,
"There's suffering. There's suffering. There's suffering."
She calmly stares at severed limbs and pleading eyes
for several seconds, then goes off to eat or play.
I make a note and slide it in with her first word, first steps,
first lock of hair. Fifteen years pass and I
don't need the book to tell me what she saw that day,
still grateful she moved on and never required me to explain.

FONT

FOR PIPPA, AT THREE

Last year two feet of clear salt water nearly killed you.
Called from where I read, I saw you bobbing
after air, and your grandmother who was watching you
swimming forty feet away.

We'd baptized you already, on All Saints'—
it's supposed to wash out devils—
salt on an infant's tongue, water on the forehead.
Perhaps the devil we drive out remains, and waits.

This year you pulled the font down on your chest.
full for other baptisms, it drenched your dress
and struck a passage open near your lungs
so every breath filled up your skin with air.

Last year we bought you water wings. We filled them
with the air we breathed. You wore them
with your lifejacket and tube until
you trusted us to hold you.

Your first nine months (and some—you liked
the water that I bore you in a bit too much)
you swam untroubled by the need to breathe.
Then you swam out, unwillingly.

The font's a bowl for water, nothing more.
The womb's a private ocean, nothing more.
The ocean's just another body's womb, nothing more.
I am the reaching, waiting shore.

REARING THE CHILDREN

I.

In a haven off the coast of Maine
puffins bury their nests,
dig out their ripened young,
stuff the yawning beaks with fish,
then abandon them.

II.

The first event my husband can recall
is sitting, diapered, at a party where,
roseate and frustrated among the adult legs,
he smacked the floor to make the people look at him.
His parents' hands, their deaf friends' hands
swooped and carved the air above.
Their talk made frantic by its unaccustomed ease,
they couldn't bear to take their eyes away
to listen to his knee-high hands,
so he yelled at the floor.

And he stayed wordless until four and
old enough to summer with his cousins by the lake,
when he learned what spoken words were for.

III.

He takes his four-year daughter off to Haydn
intending that she grow
as rich with listening as he can feed her.
And when she's had her fill of requiems and heroes,
she falls asleep along his arm
and leaves him to the massed sufficient sounds.

FINDING WATERS

I.

The rivers of Germany
fall over stone steps,
between cobbled walls,
spilling from stair
to stair, whispering
among themselves,
recalling the craft
of smoothing stones,
mimicking the tended
forests they filtered
through becoming
clear. Paved channels
lace the streets of
Freiburg, border the
cathedral, order the
city, polish glass,
scold gargoyles.
German waters
repeat the sky,
echo spires and half-
timbering, masonry
and carving, fires
and lightning,
fishery and garden.

II.

But the stream at Rossakatum ambled
between banks muffled by pebbles and moss,
glassy with ease, soft-bottomed, inattentive
to swaying pines, insects, the scatter
of water rings, slow fish. We came from
long walks smelling of pine, mulch-damp sand.
He always held my hand. Best grandchild,
Best grandfather. We carried holly for wreaths,
pine cones to crackle the fire, red leaves.
He taught me the names of trees, to watch
the loblollies sway and stand, to search
the snow for green at Easter, to walk beside
a stream. In the hospital, months deep in death,
he called me mother, wife, daughter, my own name.
Rossakatum Creek calls the rains mother, the trees
children, the ocean sleep.

III.

I find other waters—a city of fountains, piazzas filled with no flood but
light gone liquid, stone floors gilded, stone walls washed brilliant. Light of
water, light through marble, light on light. I find rivers running in small
streets. Each shines its street, makes music with the name of the basin
it seeks, learns prayers locked in the stones it wore away searching for its
fountain. Each fountain frees its voices to the embrace of the colonnade,
to the stones, statues, the feet of the statues, continuously washed by new
waters. Children dive and float up, foreheads radiant with water. I come
with one river to the basin, statues, polished surfaces, and listen to each
voice—reverent and slow, young and wise—teaching that rocks bear waters,
waters carry voices, voices tell of light, and light blesses every journey.

MY FATHER'S WIFE SPEAKS OF HER GRIEF

On the phone she says her grief feels like a walk
along the beach—sometimes the ocean's calm
sometimes the waves close over her and beat her up.
I think how if this stage of grief lasts for a year,

you'd walk that beach the best part of four hundred days:
eventually your thirst would drive you to seawater.
Eventually, you'd gut and eat raw fish.
Eventually, the sun would blind you.

And then she talks about the house, my father's house,
and how when she went out to put in early plants,
the air around her swarmed with sudden bees, in thousands,
wheeling angrily around the yard, their choral buzz

as loud as trains or helicopter blades. They funneled back
into a hole she couldn't see. Exterminators came and fled,
refusing to go near the hive they said was huge, and
left professors' names to call, who came and opened up the eaves

and found three queens, a hundred thousand workers live
and another hundred thousand dead of stress,
and said the hives had been inside the roof seventy years,
most likely. I thought about my father dying

one month to the day before that birthday
and about my grandfather who also died
a month before his seventieth year began,
and smile to think the bees began to build

perhaps exactly on the day my father came to be.
She says they took the queens away to study,
wanting to know how close-bred their genes had grown,
and whether they should separate the colonies.

They wondered how far apart or close together
these bees might need to be, and where they'll be
most likely to survive and thrive,
and whether they can live at all.

She says the eaves have been left opened up
and need to stay that way for months
to let the other insects in to feast on carcasses and honey,
to clean the space more thoroughly than humans ever could.

She says the workers swarmed again
or died, distraught without their queens,
overwhelmed by too much space and light
and no one left to tend.

She says the honey ran and ran for days
down outside walls and made the stones look caramelized
or gilded, sunlit even in the rain, and sweetening the air
a mile around, sweetening the ground around the house.

My heart is a house, a stinging house, I say,
a buzzing house for bees.
My heart is a house, an opened house—

THE GOOD TWIN SPEAKS

I am the one who never sucked her thumb.
I am the one who used her scissors carefully,
the one who always did the dishes immediately,
the one who worked up to her potential.
I am the one whose hair held a curl,
who played tennis and field hockey savagely,
who liked the bushes trimmed to look like perfect teeth,
whose cabled sweaters matched my stitched-down-pleated skirts.
I am the one who spoke French like a countess.
I am the one who liked Top 40 songs, athletic boys,
paintings of nice houses, tasteful Christmas wreaths,
colonial furniture, thank-you notes.
I never wanted to be an Arthurian heroine, a cat burglar,
A geisha, a madam, a fashion designer.
I am the one who remembers birthdays.
My skin is clear.
I am not afraid of strangers, heights, or the dark.
I have several complete collections of charming objects.
I have never caused
any trouble, for anyone.
I finish what I start.
I am the one
who has never hurt your heart.

IN SUFFICIENCY

I am older, by five years, than my grandmother when she died,
brought down by the disease we share
that makes the sweetness in our blood cry foul.

And I am twice as old as one young man whose
heart stopped where he stood, refused to answer any more
his young wife, baby girl, or anything that needed it to work.

And I am eighteen years older than the love I bear my love,
who nearly died of poison in his blood, but stayed
to go on being older than I am.

And I am almost older than James Wright
when he was felled. Older than Mozart
when he had begun to get things right, and died.

For an entire year I have been older than
Father Hopkins when he saw bright wings
and doubted them and wrote his doubt
to hurt himself and hurt the eyes
of God who permits doubt.
Who else is there to hurt but that which lets things be?

SOME FATHERS AND SOME DAUGHTERS

AFTER LISEL MUELLER

The daughters of handsome fathers long to marry
men less handsome than their fathers.
The daughters' own faces disappoint them and all
The crowds who search their faces for the next
glowing generation of their fathers' heroic, graceful bones.
On the daughters' faces their fathers' rich, curved, promising lips
consume everything beneath their noses. Or
their fathers' austere, ironic lips translate ungenerously
to frettish, judging mouths that promise nothing. Over and over again
they will be mistaken for their fathers' wives.

The daughters of charming fathers stand away—
watching arrivals and departures
from the paling backgrounds of their fathers' landscapes,
knowing that the eyes that land on them will fail to light,
the hands that hesitate to stretch toward them
have known the glamoured contact of their fathers' hands.
They stammer, or don't know how to say:
Yes, I'm his daughter. Can you show me how to leave?
They never speak the languages their fathers speak.
Their fathers call them haughty, and then laugh,
ashamed, a little—grateful for the kindness of new friends
toward their awkward offspring.

The daughters of young fathers all believe
they're old enough to know what's best for both of them.
The daughters of young fathers know
they smell the raw, familiar scent of growth,
and understand the pull of skin expanding over lengthening bones.

They hear the same delirious call of "*Play*," "*Outside*,"
"*Right Now!*" their fathers think they've hidden from themselves.
The daughters of young fathers have to learn
their fathers come to fatherhood too soon and leave
their hearts and ancestries unordered and un-understood and
their daughters have no places in their stories.
The daughters of young fathers only learn the stories of their fathers'
easy, early lives—and then
the fathers die too young, still unforgivable, and leave
their daughters moving slowly in toward themselves.

ACCEPTANCE

Everything will take longer than you planned.
You will plan too many things to do
in every free day, half-day, and hour.
All the things you plan are needful,
or dutiful, or merciful, contain the possibility of failure
or bad news, or want some etiquette.
And you will be infinitely distractible by sugar,
or sex, or clearance tables,
or the quest for perfectly arranged furniture,
or deaths, or recipes. The blinds will not be hung today,
the threadbare rug will still be on the floor,
the shelf for family photos leans against the wall tonight
exactly where you left it in the morning. Thank You notes
and Get Well cards remain unwritten.
Your driver's license goes on unrenewed.
You forget again and eat before you leave the house, so
once again your bloodwork's late. You will disappoint
yourself every living, running, malingering day.
And never in your sweet, short life
will you accept these grinning facts.

COMPLINE

1st Order

As light falls and the fireflies come out, I know
There was a single evening when the dark came
Sifting down like sugar through a sieve,
Onto the grass where I ran barefoot
Catching fireflies in glass,
Letting them die
To make myself a light.

2nd Order

I am afraid of darkness and the night is always close,
Always a clawed god reaching out to close its hands
Around the earth as if to smother a lover,
Whose hands incise, each night,
The prayers I pray all day: let me not fall down these steps,
Let me remember names, appointments, courtesies,
Let me forget the day before.
Oh, keep my eyelids open to the motes of light,
In case of angels sliding through.

Devon Miller-Duggan's poems have appeared in *CutBank*,
The Indiana Review, *Hayden's Ferry Review*,
The Chattahoochee Review, and other journals.
She teaches and advises for the University of Delaware's
Honors Program. She is married to an historian
and has two grown daughters.

OTHER TITLES BY TRES CHICAS BOOKS

Rice
Joan Logghe, 2004

Water Shed
Renée Gregorio, 2004

Just Outside the Frame: Poets from the Santa Fe Poetry Broadside
edited by Miriam Bobkoff and Miriam Sagan, 2005

Big Thank You
JB Bryan, 2006

Water Shining Beyond the Fields
John Brandi, 2006

The Sound a Raven Makes
Sawnie Morris   Michelle Holland   Catherine Ferguson, 2006
WINNER OF THE 2007 NEW MEXICO BOOK AWARD FOR POETRY

Gossip
Miriam Sagan, 2007

www.treschicasbooks.com

All Tres Chicas Book titles are available directly from the publishers at
reneeclaire@cybermesa.com
joanlogghe@hotmail.com
msagan1035@aol.com
or on the web at Amazon.com
& Small Press Distribution at spdbooks.org

Kali is an aspect of the great goddess Devi, the most complex and powerful of the goddesses. Kali is one of the fiercer aspects of Devi, but nonetheless as Shiva's consort, she represents female energy. Kali's aspect is destructive and all-pervading, as she represents the power or energy of time. Her four arms represent the four directions of space identified with the complete cycle of time. Kali is beyond time, beyond fear . . . her giving hand shows she is the giver of bliss. Because she represents a stage beyond all attachment, she appears fearful to us. So, she has a dual aspect— both destroyer of all that exists and the giver of eternal peace.

This image is from drawings by women of Mithila, India.